Wonderful, Wonderful Water!!

Wonderful, Wonderful Water!!

In Poetry and Song

C.B. Sawyers-Simms

WONDERFUL, WONDERFUL WATER!!
IN POETRY AND SONG

iUniverse books may be ordered through booksellers or by contacting:

iUniverse
1663 Liberty Drive
Bloomington, IN 47403
www.iuniverse.com
844-349-9409

Because of the dynamic nature of the Internet, any web addresses or links contained in this book may have changed since publication and may no longer be valid. The views expressed in this work are solely those of the author and do not necessarily reflect the views of the publisher, and the publisher hereby disclaims any responsibility for them.

Any people depicted in stock imagery provided by Getty Images are models, and such images are being used for illustrative purposes only.
Certain stock imagery © Getty Images.

ISBN: 978-1-6632-1723-3 (sc)
ISBN: 978-1-6632-1724-0 (e)

Library of Congress Control Number: 2021901447

Print information available on the last page.

iUniverse rev. date: 01/25/2021

CONTENTS

SONGS / LYRICS

WONDERFUL! WONDERFUL WATER!

WONDERFUL! Wonderful Water!
Universal Solvent! Most Useful entity!
In colourless and endless quantity.

<u>The Dunn's River Falls & Bathing Beach</u>
St. Ann, Jamaica, West Indies.

WHICH IS MORE?

Which is more, water or land?

And where do we get Mother Nature's sand?

What is the most refreshing drink?

Yet the world's eight billion

In it could sink?

What do we use to make us clean?

For a refreshing bath—

I really mean?

HOW DO RIVERS FLOW?

Most rivers flow from north to south;

The sea touches every river's mouth.

The sea will always keep its bound,

But rivers flow from higher ground.

WHY IS THE SEA SO SALT?

No one knows why the sea is salt

And why it moves without a halt;

Why all rivers head its way

In endless flow from day to day.

BARRY'S BOAT

Barry's boat goes out to sea,

It catches fish for you and me.

When it comes again to shore,

It rests until it sails for more.

WASH YOUR HANDS

The toilet is a germsy place,

Where people go to pass their waste.

After use, you wash your hands,

Or you'll carry germs in their thousands.

The bugs will take a jolly ride,

But your life and health you'll jeopardize.

Germs can't be seen with the naked eye,

But can cause the young and old to die.

Science Lesson Taught
Grade 4, Boscobel Primary

IF WE LET THE GREEN TREES GROW!

Trees give us shade and oxygen
We dare not live without them.
They also give us healthy food
And varieties of useful wood.
If we let the green trees grow
Rivers will have an abundant flow-
No trees! No water from the sky!
And small rivers will soon run dry.

Done at: St. Ann's Bay School of Hope
(April 1997)

THE LEAFY CLOWN

The "Leafy clown" should make you smile
Because leaves are very versatile.
For art and craft, he was created
Though now he's old and dehydrated.

The funniest clown that I could choose,
Has flower hat and flower shoes
His clothes are made of dainty leaves.
He often says "Excuse me Please!"

He turns his body right side up -
Then dives into a drinking cup!
Such clever things he does for fun
And makes us laugh till his tricks are done

He goes and comes again next spring
He seems to study everything -
Surprised! His legs are made of stems
With them he flicks before his friends.

My funny clown, he loves the town!
He looks at people upside down -
Of all the cutest things I know
He is the funniest one that grow.

MY WATER BABIES (A)

These dainty water babies
Bloom freely in the wild,
Survived throughout the ages,
And in my garden Mild

Lilly in my water garden,
Blooming night and day;
Folds its velvet petals,
Before the noontide ray.
But silent hours e're midnight,
Those petals unfold again,
For when we thought it folds to die,
It opens up its eye.

MY WATER BABIES (B) (CONT.)

The rarest Water Lilly
Has a very short day.
It spreads its rarest beauty,
To cheer us on our way:
But soon, the velvet petals
Start closing before noon,
We sigh and wonder why
The bloom is gone so soon.
But in the Maker's secret
It opens again at night
Renewed, to bless and cheer us,
In the pleasant morning light.

MY WATER BABIES (C) (CONT.)

It never blooms in the midday fair
It never sees the setting sun,
It spreads its sweetness in the mid-night air
New life for it has just begun.

MY WATER BABIES (D) (CONT.)

THE WATER HYACINTH

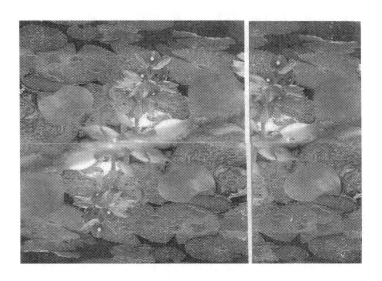

Hyacinth in the water, is always fresh and green:
The source of all its freshness, is the ever-running stream.
Soon its flower blooms and dies,
But its beauty meets the eyes,
In lavender and yellow, bedded in shades of blue––
And its spongy, bulby, stems, in colours of rarest hue.

<u>*Baby's Bottle*</u>

Boil the baby's nipple bottle,

Cover it from flies.

For baby's health and goodness sake,

No clean wash, and dirty dries!

WASH YOUR HANDS BEFORE YOU EAT

Wash your hands before you eat,
Yes, your hands! Not your feet.
Soiled feet won't kill, but dirty hands will.
On dirty hands germs like to stay,
With soap and water wash them away!

SEA POOLS

I went to have some leisure, while the others went to fish;
But I ended having treasure––better spot I couldn't wish.
I pray they'd catch a big one, their efforts to repay,
While I wandered on the rocks, with a sack to mark my way.

Continued

In amazement and in awe', I viewed from left to right;
For my newly––found sea pools, were such a pleasant sight.
There were deep pools in the rocks, there
were shallow pools as well,

There were big ones, there were small ones,
Nature's art can no one tell.

Some were empty, some were full, in others
the waves would dash and pull;
Some made tunnels underground, for
some no bottom could be found.
Some had clams, and some had crabs, some
had sea——eggs, some, empty shells;
Some had sea-weeds, some had moss, but one
had an oyster that shone like glass.

When the tide is rising high, waves would
dash beyond their bounds;
Bearing bounty, shells or prey——anything found in their way.
In one pool I found a bottle, in another a battered cent,
Things and creatures the wide world over,
their final days there to be spent.

Some shallow pools were white as snow,
and who on earth could ever know
These pools had salt and flaky brine, to
recompense my leisure time?
Come this summer if you choose, to "Idle-
A-While" for that's its name;
Such unique pools, such precious pools, no
shore on earth is quite the same.

Written for the Grade 10ᴴ students-
Oracabessa Secondary School.

THE THIRD DAY'S CREATION

On the third day, the waters were divided from the dry land.
And kept their bounds from the wide watered strand.
Also, the green herbs and every tree
Were created that day - before you and me.

THE FLOOD
GENESIS 6&7

1. Who could believe that
men were so vile
that the Holy God frowned,
and with them could not
smile?
He swore He'd destroy
them with a terrible flood,
But they doubted very
much that He ever could!

He instructed Noah to build
an ark
and on the dry land let the
vessel park
until all preparations were
made;
yet the vile people to God
never, never prayed

2. Two by two the animals went-
yes, two by two, into the ark they were sent.
God smiled on them and saved their lives,
With Mr. & Mrs. Noah, their sons and their wives

7:11; God opened up the windows of Heaven
And all the fountains of the great deep were broken!
All the evil people drowned!
Because the Holy God frowned!

WHY DO YOU ROAR, PRETTY WATER?

Why do you roar, pretty water?
You dash out sea-eggs, toss up weeds-
Disturb the spawn and whales; you care not for the living things
With shells and fins and scales;
You rock the ships! You toss the boats
You try to climb up high!
You send your currents east and west-
And end up with a giant crest.

Why do you roar, pretty water?
You roar and roar both night and day
We feel no harm for the steadfast rock
Just keep your foams at bay.
But you toss the stones and scoop out holes
And scatter all the sand-
I wonder when you'd pass the shore and come upon the land?
You tried and drifted to touch the sky
You rise and mount up oh so high!

Why do you roar, pretty water?
You hurl the driftwood thru' the air,
Which land upon some rock;
We mortals here on Earth can't dare-
(Such wisdom we do lack)
To tell what country, or what town,
You made the driftwood roam.

But this we know - from east and west, from north and south,
You take in all the waters, from all the rivers' mouth.

Continued

Why do you roar, pretty water? I think I see at last-
You cannot dare to stagnant be, with the many rivers' store;
You must mix and purge, and dash and wash
'Till you're clean as you were before.
The purity of the water, and the saltiness of the sea,
Are enjoyed by man, both rich and poor,
And of creatures wild and free,
So now your seeming anger, and disturbance by the shore,
Will not be looked at lightly, but considered as a cure.

Why do you roar, pretty water?
Your white and foamy mountains, are pushed up by the winds,
You ride, you dive, you spread out wide-
You push you pull you come back full
With thousands of soaring tides.
The wind or wave is master? It is hard for one to tell:
But the mighty, mighty struggle, cause the waves to beat and swell.
The water gives its final blow, when it reaches to its bound,
And send the wind with a gushing sound, on all the isle around.

I'm glad I know, pretty water, why you thunder and you roar!
You're part of the world's five oceans, and
of dozens of seas and more.
You mix the hot waves and the cold, and bring them to our feet;
And when you're clean and calm again, we'll taste your waters sweet.
I thank you for the cooling winds, you're forced to come to shore.
We can't but sing your praises, as the breeze bangs on our door;

No need for cooling measures, for nature surely knows,
The sea will send refreshing winds, whatever place it flows.
The sea will send refreshing winds, whatever place it flows.

Written March 30, 1979
& appreciated by Grade 10[H] students,
Oracabessa Secondary

CHAMBERS PEN!

Chambers Pen! You wouldn't believe!
How much I sighed! How much I grieved!
'Twas here I was taught to make my weekly scheme.
And alas! 'twas the first and last "Eisteddfod" I'd seen.
Chambers Pen! My very first school!
I regret I had to leave you so soon!
When I left on that Friday, I felt quite bereft,
With TEARS of departing mingled with joy
To witness the arrival of my sister's baby boy –
Believe it or not! He's the one on the left.

When mi memba Chambers Pen
Wata come a mi yie.

CHAMBERS PEN CONT'D

Middle Division Classes combined – shared by
Willoughby Harvey & myself (1956)

WHO?

1.

Who caused the cool refreshing dew
To water everything that grew
Made rivers flow, and the deep blue sea
For man and beast, who were yet to be?

2.

Who made the sun and crystal rain
To ripen the harvest golden grain
Washing drains, kissing flowers
Cleansing all the plants and bowers?

3.
Who made the moon and stars to shine
For times and seasons so divine
The sun by day, and the moon by night?
The great Creator made all things right.

THE FLOWER CLOWN
designed by Andrea Sawyers

The Flower Clown has come to town
And never wears a frown:
He has a red cap on his head
Bedecked with colours
from the flower bed.

He feeds on water and dewdrops pure,
And never, never asks for more;
His frilly clothes that bloom in June
Are the yellow poi that falls too soon.

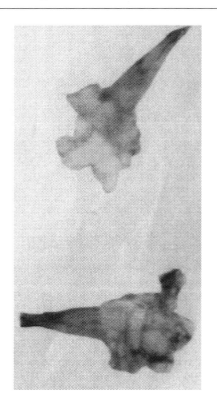

SEEDY POND IN WESTMORELAND

The Seedy Pond is a dangerous spot
Tho' fish abound in it a lot.
It was so attractive to our school boys
For they preferred to fish than to play with toys.
Fay Mercurius became very curious
And Inez Wright said, "We're in a great plight!"
The pond by the school did not even have a name-
It had no history; it had no fame!
"But it's safer by far" said Ezra Kerr.
So, Mrs. Mercurius, the current head,
Had a dialogue with the Ministry of Ed.,
(And in no time, they made a quick fix.)
Surprising, one day a truck came down the road
Filled with drums- a very heavy load.
It turned right in the Barneyside School
That teachers and pupils couldn't keep their cool.
When the truck unloaded its precious prize
We all could not believe our very eyes!
"Kirkwood" and gold fish all-different "size" –
Were thrown in the pond by those very strong guys.
Our boys went to fish in Seedy no more
For they had abundance of fish next door

N.B. "Kirkwood" or black fish, so named, as Mr.
Kirkwood introduced it to Westmoreland.

THE UNDERGROUND LAKE

1.

Have you ever gone sailing on the underground lake?
Have you at any time its cool waters take?
Have you ever listened to the musical rocks
(As you pass by in the boat)
Playing tunes in every key, and in every single note?
Have you seen the blind fish that in this lake are found
That live a happy wild life, two hundred feet underground?
To be candid. I did.

2.

Have you ever been in gross darkness that you think you have no eyes?
I mean in the Runaway Caves, where you cannot see the skies.
Have you ever heard the tour guide say, "Nerve up for the dark."
And after a brief black-out
Everyone respond with a shout?
To be candid, I did.
'Tis not a fantasy or fake!
It's a real underground lake.

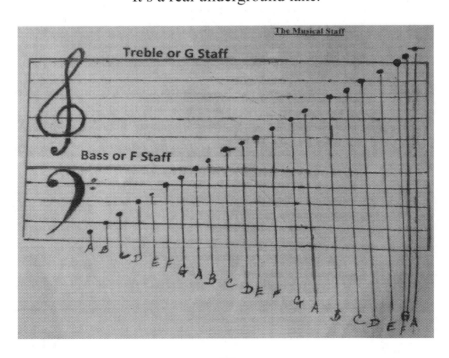

29

THE BLUE LAGOON
(BLUE HOLE) (180 FT. DEEP)

It's not a small pond, it's not a shallow lake
it's not a true lagoon-I pray my word you'll take.
They say it's a bottomless hole, of deep waters blue-
varying at times to shades of Blue-green hue.
'Tis a rare mixture of three waters in one,
A blend from creation that's second to none-
Our mini "Mariana" of the Island in the sun.
A source of sea water through a narrow funnel
Integrating with fresh water from an underground tunnel
Plus one of the most wonderful! wonderful Things!
Streams of liquid compound from mineral springs
All these still waters come to our feet
Some swim and taste of its blue waters sweet
But never dive! O never so brave!
Fearing they'd be conducted by the mythical Mermaid
To her mysterious dwelling in underground caves.

Dragons inhabit the water they say,
But it's glimpses of rear deep-water fish far away -
Enjoying their "paradise", but to us unknown-
Wild, colourful, mysterious and quite overgrown.
It's one of the most beautiful and enchanted spots
That makes Portland famous among the haves and the have nots.
The famous Brooke Shields' movie made this blue hole come alive!
Plus, the well publicized site for the Jacques Cousteau dive.
It's one of the legendary beauty spots of the world,
Everyone should enjoy it-the young and the old.
Where ever you are, you can't come too soon
To this enchanted site-The Blue lagoon
A natural favourite for swimmers; but if you choose not to float
You'll Be safely carried on a Maritime boat.
Where ever you are, you can't come too soon
To this enchanted site-The Blue lagoon

BAPTISED IN THE HEALING STREAM

Chant / Song
"Dip dem, Bedwod, dip dem!
Dip dem in a healing stream;
Dip dem sweet but na dip dem deep,
Dip some-a-dem, fi dem aching feet!

Some come from the north,
Some come from the south,
Some a-dem come from all round about.

O! Dip dem, Bedwod, dip dem!
Dip dem in a healing stream;
Dip dem sweet but na dip dem deep,
Dip some-a-dem, fi dem aching feet!" etc.

Alexander Bedward, from the Baptist Church moved away-
He started a revivalist movement – the healing stream, made his day.
This charismatic African – Jamaican from St. Andrew hill
The whole Jamaica with excitement fill!
The movement was arousing, sensational – new
From all walks of life, the people to August Town drew;
Virtue they said, was in the healing stream.
So the sun was never set at the August Town scene

Boarding in River's Dale at age nineteen,
My mother was caught up in the crowd as a teen
For to see and hear Alexander Bedward;
For tho' the water could not wash her soul clean
He dipped her once, in the healing stream.

When her parents collected her that night –
She was already a Bedwardite.
Fellow Jamaicans, I want you to know –
That the stream dried up a long time ago –
But the rich history and awakening can no man erase,
'Till all of us – God's children, see His wonderful face.
Yes! The crowd ran after a "one-man team"
To be baptised in the healing stream.

THE MARIANA TRENCH - 35,000 FT DEEP

It's the deepest water hole in all of
the five oceans of the world.
Brave men dared to fathom its' depts,
While spectators held their anxious
breath –
They reached their goal for history's sake,
But nothing could from Mariana take.
O yes! Oh yes! 'twas all in vain,
'Til Cameron dared to try again.
In his solo sub, he took a dive -
We feared he'd not return alive!
But his submarine with bionic arms
Grabbed what it could, with its magic palms.
He returned with triumph from the belly of hell
With shots of Pacific's deep wonders as well.

James Cameron filmed the Titanic woe,
(that new ship that sank a century ago.)
Impressed by the loss of precious lives
He showed to the world the agony; the
cries -
On the Atlantic before the ship went down.
While the ship was going down,
Flashed a spark of hope! that God their
souls could save

Before they sank beneath the waves -
to their watery graves.
They sang a song of hope! "Nearer, my
God, to Thee, Nearer to Thee!
E'en though it be a cross, That raiseth me.
Still all my song shall be, nearer, my
God, to Thee, nearer, my God, to Thee,
nearer to Thee!
Though like the wanderer, The sun gone
down,

Darkness be over me, My rest a stone,
Yet in my dreams I'd be, nearer, my God,
to Thee, nearer, my God, to Thee,
nearer to Thee!

There let the way appear, steps unto Heaven;
All that thou sendest me in mercy given:
Angels to beckon me, nearer, my God, to
Thee, nearer, my God, to Thee,
nearer to Thee!
Then with my waking thoughts, bright with thy praise
Out of my stony griefs, Bethel I'll raise;
So by my woes to be, nearer, my God, to
Thee, nearer, my God, to Thee,
nearer to Thee!
Or if, on joyful wing, cleaving the sky,
Sun, moon, and stars forgot, upward I fly,
Still all my song shall be nearer, my God,
to Thee, nearer, my God, to Thee,
nearer to Thee!

**Still all my song shall be nearer, my God,
to Thee, nearer, my God, to Thee,
nearer to Thee!"
Cameron to the deep Pacific did go,
Inspired by the history of Titanic woe.**

NB. James Cameron dived to the Mariana Trench
March 2012 - 100 years after Titanic Sank

PORT MARIA SCHOOL OF HOPE

1

Port Maria School of Hope-
I give you a shout!
Sorry The Sandy storm water washed you out!
Happy you're now sheltered in the Port Maria Baptist Church-
Sincerely hope you'll not only perch,
But settle In the very church-
Where your ancestors went to school.
Thanks to the Baptists for opening their arms again
So our children can be educated, and skilfully use the pen.
Also grateful indeed to the Catholic Church-
Our beloved Lady Star of the Sea-
For hosting our school, and helping to make education free.
We only regret that the Sandy Storm water, plus its wears and tears,
Have put you in such a terrible lurch.
In 1838, when slavery was abolished,
Queen Victoria, every household with a Holy Bible furnished.

2

But alas! neither parents nor children could read!
Now that they could choose their destiny,
Now that they were freed:
But good news followed the Bibles-
Queen Victoria sent English recruits.
And the efforts bore much fruits.
Although there were no schools in our island then,
And the children had no pencils or pen,

The missionary recruits came with a plan
To educate every boy and girl in our land.
They gathered all the children, and opened up the doors
Of all the existing churches in the circuits, districts and cures.
So the kids sat on the benches, and were taught to read and write:
Much to everyone's great pleasure, and very sweet delight.
But look! did you know that the Holy Bible
Was our first reading book?

(a) **History**

1. The Port Maria Baptist Church was built in 1828- ten years before the abolition of slavery in Jamaica.

2. Hurricane Sandy hit Jamaica on October 24, 2012. The eastern section of the island suffered most. The Sandy storm water deluged the town of Port Maria, however, the Kirk United Church, (former-Presbyterian) the Baptist and Anglican churches did not suffer severely because of their elevation and sites on the outskirts of the town.

(b) Activity Corner

If the All-Age or Primary School in your area is on a church compound, write the name of the church

(c) History in a nutshell

A. Our first school was the church.
B. Our first reading book was the Bible
C. Our first teachers were English missionaries

If the all-age or primary school in your community is not in a church yard, find out from the older folks in your community which church compound the original elementary school was located and write the name of that church in the space provided.

(d) Example Of Seven (7) Churches In Jamaica Which Were Built Before The Abolition of Slavery and Used As Some of Our First Schools

	Church	Parish	Year
1.	Port Maria Anglican Church (original building)	St. Mary	1689
2.	Lucea Baptist Church	Hanover	1827

3.	Port Maria Baptist Church	St. Mary	1828
4.	Gurney's Mt. Baptist Church	Hanover	1830
5.	Pt. Maria Presbyterian Church	St. Mary	1832
6.	Bethlehem Moravian Church	St. Elizabeth	1833
7.	Mt. Ward Methodist Church	Hanover	1834

Snap Shot
Graduation 2014
Performing 'I have a Dream'

Sunshine School of Hope (now Edgehill School of Special Education)

Dr. John E. McDowell, O.D., J.P., B.D.S (Edin.)
First Chairman: Sunshine School of Hope.
Still active at 92 in 2015

MEMOIRS OF THE CALEDONIA SCHOOL, WESTMORELAND

My stay was very short - I went to and fro-
But my memory will not let you go.
The musical instruments you made by hand,
Stand out in my mind, and the musical band.

O Caledonia! It's refreshing to remember
The fresh watercress and peculiar God-a-mi fish,
Which abound in your Cabaritta River.
Christmas dinner was delightful with that fish-
Served with water cress – a delicious dish.
O Caledonia! I'll sing your praise
When I remember those golden days.

NB God-A-Mi-Fish is peculiar to the Cabaritta River

MEMORY TRAINING MUSICAL INSTRUMENTS (TRADITIONAL)

1.

O! we can play on the big bass drum
And this is the way we do it:
Rig – dig – bum, is the big bass drum
And this is the way we do it:

2.

O! we can play on the castanet,
And this is the way we do it:
Ticka – ticka- ticka is the castanet,
And rig – dig – bum, is the big bass drum
And this is the way we do it:

3.

O! we can play on the bugle horn,
And this is the way we do it:
Tam – ta – ta – ra is the bugle horn
And ticka – ticka- ticka is the castanet,
And rig – dig – bum, is the big bass drum
And this is the way we do it:

4.

O! we can play on the kettle drum
And this is the way we do it:
Tittle – tittle – tittle is the kettle drum,
And tam – ta – ta – ra is the bugle horn

And ticka – ticka- ticka is the castanet,
And rig – dig – bum, is the big bass drum
And this is the way we do it:

5.
O! we can play on the double bass
And this is the way we do it:
Zoom – zoom – zoom is the double bass
And tittle – tittle – tittle is the kettle drum,
And tam – ta – ta – ra is the bugle horn
And ticka – ticka- ticka is the castanet,
And rig – dig – bum, is the big bass drum
And this is the way we do it:

WONDERFUL WINDSOR
WATER ON FIRE!!

A Maroon Maiden neat and clean,
Went down to a running stream,
When she espied a wasp nest on an overhanging tree
And decided to light it with fire!
The burning nest fell in the stream and set
the water a-blaze!
So, she rushed up the hill to her mother-
A true alarm to raise!
This wonderful, wonderful "thing" turned out
to be a mineral spring.
Said the mother to her daughter,
"We'll name it the Windsor Fire Water!"

Windsor
St. Ann's Bay
St. Ann
Jamaica W.I.

This Maroon Maiden is now a Dame-
Malia Taylor, her honourable name.
'Twas in nineteen twenty two
When she made her discovery new.
She's been dipping in the spring for ninety
years and more-
Now at one hundred and eleven
The warm water is brought to her door.
It keeps her fit as a fiddle, and that isn't any
riddle-
For the "Jewel" she has found,
Is still bubbling from underground

Math Corner
Mrs. Taylor was 111 years in 2013.
When was she born? _____

How old would she be
in the following:

2012- _____
2014- _____
2016- _____
2018- _____
2021- _____
2022- _____
2050- _____
2052- _____

NB: The Flames can be lit and extinguished as desired
Only at the spot above the bubbles, to be admired,
Or to cook a pot-at this hot spot.

At the Fire Water with Friends- 2013

DELESSEPS' TWINS –
TEN YEARS APART

DeLesseps the French man viewed the piece of land
That separated the Mediterranean from the Red Sea;
When an idea was born, and to the French people, made an
urgent plea.
"If I open up a waterway' said he,
Between the Mediterranean and the Red Sea,
Then ships a toll would pay to sail this very short way.
So if you'll quickly invest, I'll guarantee you an handsome
interest:
Besides, you'll be saving time and lives,
As maritime merchants will return safely
To their children and their wives."

Said the French people in response, "What a splendid idea-wow!
This new water way will create prosperity:
we'll invest the money now!"
So in 1859, the French held up Lesseps' hand:
They started on the project to cut the piece of land.
'Twas very hard work using shovels and
buckets to remove great loads of sand,
But on November 17, 1869, the Suez Canal
was completed: one of the most
creative of the 19th century masterpieces -
(Engineer Lesseps' Invention)
The Suez Canal was such a resounding success
That 10 years later, DeLesseps to Panama progressed.

His second brainchild in the New World was born
So ships could say "goodbye" to long and dangerous 'Cape Horn'.
The French and fellow Europeans invested in it as well-
But little did they know, mosquitoes would give them hell.
The Engineer and his merry men, made a successful start-
But mosquitoes! mosquitoes! broke DeLesseps' heart:
Yellow fever from mosquito bites, killed most of his men,
So he was forced to shut down the project and flee then.
"Broken hearted!" he cried,
He returned to France and died.
DeLesseps' twins – ten years apart –
The second twin that broke his heart.
If he knew then, that his child could revive
At that time, he might not have died.

Continued

America waged war in this treacherous Gulf –
(Yes! In the Gulf of Mosquitos, that caused
much sorrow much woes;)
By finding a way to combat those foes;
Plus calling for thousands of Caribbean recruits
To help to kill those little "brutes".
Even some of our third year scholars
Were enlisted in the "army" - they earned U.S. dollars.
America won that bitter war! We hail her as the Western star!
For not only the mosquitoes she defeated,
But the Panama Canal she also completed.
In the year 1914 when the First World War broke out*
The new canal was opened, and ships found a very short route*
O! If Ferdinand DeLesseps could only know!
That his second brainchild is now on the go!

Expansion! Expansion! On this key water way –
Are the plans now a-foot - the talk of the day.
More business, more ships, sail boats too, and the powerful tug,
With Jamaica in mid waters as the Caribbean hub.
I hail! I Christen! I now wage war-
And claim DeLesseps as the 19th century European Star!

<u>Ode To Manning Marsh</u>

ODE TO MANNING MARSH

He hailed from the hills of St.
Mary,
Had lots of fruits and dairy;
His smiles were always so cheery
And he was never, never weary
To master the guitar at the Mico,
Teach the piccolo in school,
And observe the Golden Rule.
He was a Mozart as headmaster,
A Bach in the Anglican cure,
He played such melodious tunes-
But those tunes are heard no more.
Ode to Manning Marsh,
It was so sudden and harsh!
We have no power to turn the clock,
Or Rivers of tears would bring him
back.
Oh! If rivers of tears could bring
him back!!!

SONGS / LYRICS

LULLABY
DREAM SWEET DREAMS, MY BABY

Sleep, baby sleep, don't stare or weep;
Daddy is out on the ocean deep.
Daddy is out on the far away sea,
Daddy will come back to you and me.

Close your bright eyes baby,
Dream of the mermaid lady;
Daddy will bring her golden comb,
Whenever your daddy comes back home.

But there's no mermaid lady,
There is no golden comb,
So, dream sweet dreams my baby,
For surely your Daddy will soon come home.

WHO GAVE THE NIGHTINGALE ITS TUNE? (A)

1.

Who gave the nightingale its tune?
Put the light into the moon
Ordered morning, night and noon
Make all lovely flowers bloom?

    Refrain: Omnipotent! The Holy One –
    Created these, 'ere he made man

2.

Who sent the cool refreshing shower,
Made the day and every hour;
Formed the world with his mighty power,
Planted Eden without a sower?

3.

Who put the rainbow in the sky?
Made fish to swim and birds to fly,
Painted them in colours bright,
Much to everyone's delight?

WHO GAVE THE NIGHTINGALE ITS TUNE? (B)

Original words written June 29, 1979

1.

Who gave the nightingale its tune
Put the light into the moon
Make the flowers bloom in June
Order morning, night and noon?
> Omnipotent! The Holy One … .
> Created these, 'ere He made man (rep)

2.

Who send the dew drops on the grass
Made the beasts, and calm the ass
Formed the gold and molten brass
Preserved the world while ages past?
> Omnipotent! The Holy One … .
> Created these, 'ere He made man (rep)

3.

Who put the fragrance in the flower
Send the cool refreshing shower
Make the day and every hour
Who has this almighty power?
> Omnipotent! The Holy One … .
> Created these, 'ere He made man (rep)

4.

Who put the stars into the sky
Taught the birds and bees to fly
Guide the clouds that hurry by
Form the hills and mountains high?
   Omnipotent! The Holy One ... .
   Created these, 'ere He made man (rep)

5.

Who taught the fawn and hare to run,
Paint the clouds at setting sun
Fold the flower when day is done
Will remain when man is gone?
   Omnipotent! The Holy One ... .
   He shall remain when man is gone.

OH! LISTEN TO THE PRAISES

Words & music by Celia B. Simms,
Arranged by J. B. Williams

LOVELY RAINDROPS
FALLING DOWN

Words & Music
by
Celia B. Simms

Arranged by J. B. Williams

Crystal raindrops from on high
Kissed the plants before they die;
Then so quickly they revive,
Surely, 'tis the kiss of life.

LET ME DRINK

1.

There's a hallow in my soul, There's a cavern in my heart;
I know I'm getting cold, Please Lord Jesus don't depart.

<u>Refrain.</u>

Fill my soul with thy grace
Fill my heart with thy love
Fill my mind with thy peace
Fill my lips with thy praise.

2.

That old dragon tries to get me, he has sapped my strength and grace;
If I'm reduced to dry bones, I shall never see thy face.

3.

Keep me daily near the cross; Feed me on the bread of life;
Let me drink then face the foe, armed and strengthened for the strife.

LET'S KEEP JAMAICA FREE

Words & music by Celia B. Simms

Arranged by Joe B. Williams

Written, 1983, by Celia B. Simms
prepared for Oracabessa Secondary School
for Jamaica's 21ˢᵗ Independence

Edgehill School of Special Education, Port Maria Unit,
performing the "I have a Dream" in 2014

ABOUT THE AUTHOR

Cecelia B Sawyers-Simms is a great lover of children. She chose as a career the profession of teaching and taught for 45 years in various departments, teaching children from 41/2 years to 18 year olds in the Infant, Primary (then all age), Secondary, and School of Special Education.

She used Nursery rhymes, poetry on the whole to aid speech and memory and music to inspire learning and provide enjoyment in the various age groups she taught. Book of a Thousand Poems and other poetry books were widely used, but she composed her own poems in various subject areas such as: science, history, geography, hygiene, religious education, art & craft, nature poems and poems for pleasure. Some of the poems were memorized by her pupils.

All the poems in this book were written by her, some already used, others reflecting fond memories. All of the songs and lyrics in the second half of this book were also written by her.

This pictorial poetry book is dedicated to all the children she taught in the following schools:

1.	Chamber's Pen All Age	- Hanover
2.	Mt. Hannah All Age	- Hanover
3.	Barney side All Age	- Westmoreland
4.	Mt. Ward All Age	- Hanover
5.	Caledonia All Age	- Westmoreland
6.	Gurney's Mt All Age	- Hanover (her Alma- Mater)
7.	Falmouth Barracks All Age	- Trelawny
8.	Granville All Age	- Trelawny

9. Rio Bueno All Age   - Trelawny
10. Allman Town Infant   - Kingston
11. Watford Hill All Age   - Hanover
12. St. Peter Claver Primary   - Kingston
13. Central Branch Infant   - Kingston
14. Dunrobin Primary   - Kingston
15. Brandon Hill All Age   - St. Andrew
16. Windsor Castle All Age   - St. Portland
17. Oracabessa Secondary   - St. Mary
18. Boscobel Primary   - St. Mary
19. Mt. Angus All Age   - St. Mary
20. Sunshine School of Hope   - St. Ann
21. School of Hope- St. Mary (now Edgehill School of Special Education, Pt. Maria unit)

Boscobel, Jamaica, W.I.

The Swinging Bridge over the Otrim River
Port Maria, St. Mary (1964)

Printed in the United States
By Bookmasters